MW01079564

THE
𝒫RAISES

Psalm 148
A PSALM OF DAVID

Illustrated for children by
Niko Chocheli

ST VLADIMIR'S SEMINARY PRESS
2000

The Praises
Psalm 148, A Psalm of David

Copyright © 2000 by
St. Vladimir's Seminary Press
575 Scarsdale Rd., Crestwood, NY 10707
1-800-204-2665

All Rights Reserved

ISBN 0-88141-206-6

The publication of this book was
made possible in part due to the generosity of
Mr. & Mrs. Mark Hudoff.

Scripture excerpts are taken from the New Oxford Annotated Bible,
Revised Standard Version, copyright © 1973

No part of this book may be reproduced or transmitted in any form
or by any means, electronic or mechanical, including photocopying, recording,
or by any information storage or retrieval system, without
permission in writing from the publisher.

Cover design: Amber Houx

PRINTED IN HONG KONG

Praise the LORD!

PSALM 148

Praise the LORD!
Praise the LORD from the heavens,
   praise him in the heights!
Praise him, all his angels,
   praise him, all his host!

Praise him, sun and moon,
   praise him, all you shining stars!
Praise him, you highest heavens,
   and you waters above the heavens!

Let them praise the name of the LORD!
   For he commanded and they were created.
And he established them for ever and ever;
   he fixed their bounds which
     cannot be passed.

Praise the LORD from the earth,
   you sea monsters and all deeps,
fire and hail, snow and frost,
   stormy wind fulfilling
      his command!

Mountains and all hills,
   fruit trees and all cedars!
Beasts and all cattle,
   creeping things and
      flying birds!

Kings of the earth and all peoples,
   princes and all rulers of the earth!
Young men and maidens together,
   old men and children!

Let them praise the name of the LORD,
   for his name alone is exalted;
   his glory is above earth and heaven.
He has raised up a horn for his people,
   praise for all his saints,
   for the people of Israel who are near to him.
Praise the LORD!

Praise the LORD from the heavens,
praise him in the heights!
Praise him, all his angels,
praise him, all his host!
Praise him, sun and moon,
praise him, all you shining stars!
Let them praise the name of the LORD!

NIKO CHOCHELI.

Praise the LORD from the earth,
you sea monsters and all deeps,
Praise the LORD!

Fire and hail, snow and frost,
stormy wind fulfilling his command!
Praise the LORD!

Mountains and all hills,
fruit trees and all cedars!
Praise the LORD!

Beasts and all cattle,
Praise the LORD!

Creeping things and flying birds!
Praise the LORD!

Let them praise the name of the LORD!
For he commanded and they were created.
And he established them for ever and ever;
he fixed their bounds
which cannot be passed.

Praise the Lord!

Kings of the earth and all peoples,
princes and all rulers of the earth!
Praise the LORD!

Young men and maidens together,
old men and children,
Praise the LORD!

Let them praise the name of the LORD,
for his name alone is exalted;
his glory is above earth and heaven.
He has raised up a horn for his people,
praise for all his saints, for the people of
Israel who are near to him.
Praise the LORD!

Praise the Lord!

Psalms 148 and 150 each begin with the words "Praise the Lord!" For this reason these psalms are traditionally called "the Praises". They are always chanted toward the end of the Church's morning service called Matins. In Western churches this part of the morning prayer is simply called *Lauds*, the Latin word for *Praises*.

As is so powerfully and marvelously illustrated in this present book, *The Praises* invite everyone and everything in the whole creation to praise the Lord. The angels and animals and natural elements, with every living thing headed and cared for by human beings of every age, gender, class and nation, are commanded to sing and dance and make melody to the Creator of all.

Christians believe that God creates everyone and everything through his only Son Jesus Christ. Indeed, as the apostle Paul teaches, all things are not only created by Jesus, but they are made in him and through him who is before all things and in whom all things hold together. (Colossians 1:15-17, Hebrews 1:1-1)

The apostle John identifies Jesus with God's divine Word by whom all things were made (John 1:1-3), a teaching directly cited in the Church's baptismal and eucharistic Symbol of Faith, the Nicene-Constantinopolital Creed.

Before the *Praises* are chanted at Matins, the Orthodox priest silently says this prayer. As we praise the Lord through this present book of illustrations, may this prayer be ours as well.

> O God, our God, who has brought into being by Your will all the powers endowed with speech and reason, we beg and beseech You to accept our Praises which, together with all your creatures, we now offer according to our strength. Reward us with the rich gifts of Your goodness. For to You every knee bows down, in heaven and on earth and under the earth, and every breath, and every created being, sings Your ineffable glory, for You alone are the true and most merciful God. All heavenly powers praise You, and to You we also send up glory, to the Father and to the Son and to the Holy Spirit, now and ever and unto ages of ages. Amen.

Fr. Thomas Hopko
Dean, St Vladimir's Orthodox Seminary

ARTIST'S ACKNOWLEDGEMENTS

I devote this work to the memory of my grandmother, Tamara, who was the constant inspiration of my formative years.

I am deeply grateful for the blessing of this book by His Holiness Ilia II, Catholicos-Patriarch of all Georgia. I would like to thank St. Philip's Antiochian Orthodox Church, which has been and will remain my true guide in life, as well as a spiritual connection to my Georgian Orthodox Christian roots.

I thank my parents, Robert and Leila, who have always given me their loving support. They sent their only child off to America to pursue an international art career and to teach in the honor of the old masters. The spirit of the sacrifice they made by encouraging me to leave my home in the Republic of Georgia for a new life in the United States fills me each day.

I thank the many friends who have enabled me to remain in the United States through their on-going efforts on my behalf. Without their prayers and love, with which I continue to be surrounded, none of this would have been been possible.

And lastly, I thank Kristen, my fiancée, who is always by my side.

Glory be to God!